MORNINGTON PENINSULA
BATHEDINCOLOUR

ANNE MONTEITH
BRYCE DUNKLEY

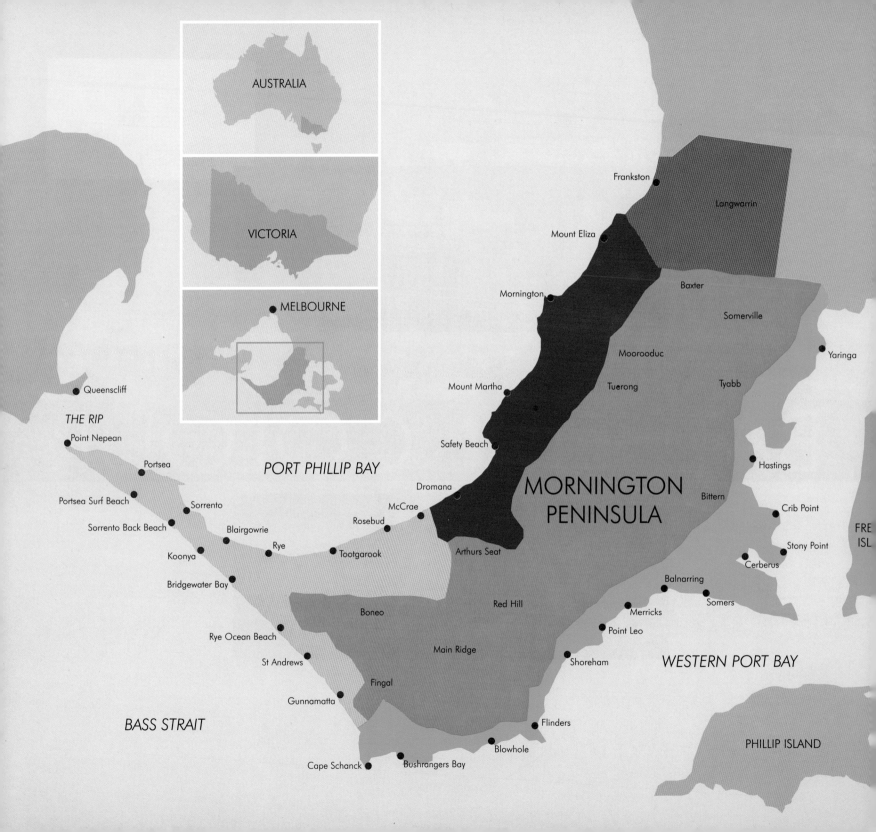

AUSTRALIA

VICTORIA

MELBOURNE

THE RIP

Queenscliff

Point Nepean

Portsea

Portsea Surf Beach

Sorrento

Sorrento Back Beach

Blairgowrie

Koonya

Rye

Bridgewater Bay

Tootgarook

PORT PHILLIP BAY

McCrae

Rosebud

Dromana

Arthurs Seat

Rye Ocean Beach

St Andrews

Boneo

Fingal

Gunnamatta

BASS STRAIT

Cape Schanck

Bushrangers Bay

Blowhole

Frankston

Langwarrin

Mount Eliza

Mornington

Baxter

Somerville

Moorooduc

Mount Martha

Tuerong

Tyabb

Yaringa

Safety Beach

MORNINGTON
PENINSULA

Hastings

Bittern

Crib Point

Stony Point

Cerberus

FRE
ISL

Balnarring

Red Hill

Somers

Merricks

Point Leo

Main Ridge

WESTERN PORT BAY

Shoreham

Flinders

PHILLIP ISLAND

NORTHERN

Journey along Mornington Peninsula's northern coastline on Port Phillip Bay and be introduced to charming seaside towns that express a sense of distinct identity — Mount Eliza, Mornington, Mount Martha, Safety Beach and Dromana. An exclusive air surrounds Mount Eliza — prestigious homes and beautiful gardens amidst rustic native vegetation; streets designed by Walter Burleigh Griffin (renowned for his design of Canberra, Australia's capital city), coastal cliffs and secluded bays; colourful bathing boxes and vineyards.

Mornington is a vibrant, bayside location noted for its popular events and unique features — a beautiful harbour and yacht club; coastline of red bluffs and beaches; historic buildings, specialty shops and eateries. A change of pace distinguishes Mount Martha, a tranquil and picturesque hamlet nestling between steep cliffs. South Beach is one of the Peninsula's most memorable beaches. The long sweep of golden sand is a spectacular background for 239 colourful beach boxes.

The scenic drive along a winding, cliff-top Esplanade links Mount Martha to Safety Beach, home to the Coast Guard and new marina. Safety Beach marks the start of the almost unbroken sweep of popular, sandy beaches to the south. Dromana is the bustling and colourful holiday destination whose early growth was attributable to the building of a pier that opened up the area to trade and tourism. Dromana was one of the first foreshores to cater for holiday makers in `tent cities`.

Arthurs Seat is the highest point on the Mornington Peninsula overlooking Dromana and the vast expanse of Port Phillip Bay. Small islands, lighthouses, a man-made fort, navigation aids, beacons and buoys delineate the shipping channels used by more than seven thousand ship-visits annually. The steep, winding road to the summit passes spectacular viewing bays marked by historical plaques commemorating early navigators; culminating at the chairlift, craft cottages, galleries, maze and walking trails in Arthurs Seat State Park.

Photo: Beach boxes, Mount Martha

MOUNT ELIZA

Mount Eliza portrays a stylish neighbourhood with a scenic foreshore of secluded bays and beaches. Prestigious homes nestled among native vegetation and exquisite gardens dominate the eroding cliffs and inquisitive visitors succumb to the air of secrecy in an exclusive location.

Canadian Bay

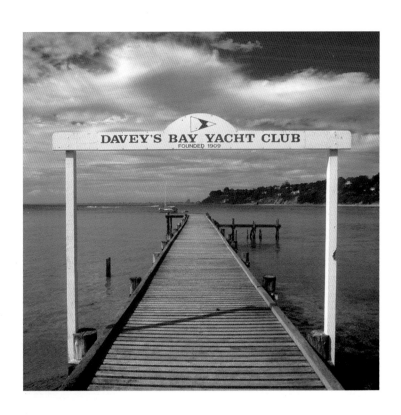

Daveys Bay Yacht Club

Bathing boxes, Ranelagh Beach

Mornington Yacht Club and The Rocks Restaurant

MORNINGTON HARBOUR

Overlooking Port Phillip Bay with distant views of Melbourne's skyline, Mornington is the largest town on the Peninsula. Beautiful historic buildings, abundant cafes and traditional street markets contribute to the charm and vibrancy of the distinctly maritime settlement.

The natural deep harbour at Schnapper Point is home to one of the largest and most technically advanced ocean racing yachts in the world. Skandia Wild Thing took line honours in the Sydney-Hobart sailing classic in December 2003. The maxi was designed, built and skippered by locals while half the crew comprised Mornington Yacht Club members.

Mothers Beach

MORNINGTON BEACHES

Every bay beach has a distinctive character – Mills Beach, Mothers Beach, Shire Hall Beach, Scout Hall Beach, Royal Beach, Fossil Beach and Fishermans Beach. Some possess remnants of days gone by – weathered stone steps, fossils, a fraying sea wall and fresh fish sales, while others provide modern amenities, boat hire, kiosk and safe swimming afforded by protection from the popular pier. Mornington beaches sparkle with the presence of 175 colourful bathing boxes set against a backdrop of striking red bluffs.

Mornington Harbour

Bathing boxes, Mornington

Mornington Cup

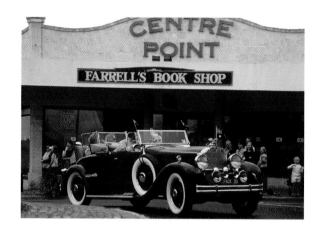

Hunts Club, Country Life Festival

Australia Day Parade

The Royal Hotel built in 1857

Post Office Museum

Grand Hotel

Main Street Clock Tower

Historic Mornington Park

Mount Martha

MOUNT MARTHA

Mount Martha is a picturesque hamlet with inspiring coastal scenery. Steep cliffs in the north give way to broad, golden beaches and colourful bathing boxes in the south. Rugged coast resumes for six kilometres along The Esplanade where anglers perch precariously and swimmers dive from the cliff tops or snorkel in clear waters below. Mount Martha's bathing boxes are brightly coloured with gabled roofs and awnings while at Dromana many boxes display decorative artwork (top photo).

Mount Martha South Beach

Safety Beach

DROMANA

Dromana nestles at the foot of Arthurs Seat `where the mountain meets the sea´. The building of the pier in 1873 established Dromana as a commercial hub for the area and a popular tourist destination. Every summer the inviting stretch of shallow, sandy beach entices the return of campers to tent cities on the foreshore.

Heronswood (circa 1871), Dromana

HISTORIC HOMESTEADS

Heronswood, registered by the National Trust and described as Gothic Revival, is constructed from local granite with limestone dressings and bell-shaped roof. The imposing property is home to The Diggers Club, Australia's largest gardening club.

Historic homesteads at McCrae, Briars Park, Ballam Park, Mulberry Hill, Beleura and Coolart provide valuable insight into the lifestyle of early settlers on the Mornington Peninsula.

DROMANA DRIVE-IN

The family operated Drive-in celebrated its fortieth birthday in 2002 with the opening of a third screen and a `sixties diner´. Defying the world trend of closing `soft top cinemas´, this drive-in has operated continuously since 1963.

Geodetic dial, Arthurs Seat summit

Seawinds, Arthurs Seat State Park

Entrance to Port Phillip Bay viewed from Chapmans Point Lookout

Arthurs Seat III and Old Viewing Tower

William Ricketts sculpture

Seawinds boardwalk

Arthurs Seat Chairlift

ARTHURS SEAT

Arthurs Seat is the highest peak (305 metres) on the Mornington Peninsula and commands spectacular views of Port Phillip Bay, Western Port Bay, French Island and Phillip Island. The Arthurs Seat Chairlift was opened in 1960. Victoria's longest chairlift is one kilometre long with a ride taking twenty minutes to reach the summit.

The southern coastline links an eclectic mix of bayside towns and ocean beaches – McCrae, Rosebud, Tootgarook, Rye, Blairgowrie, Sorrento, Portsea, Port Nepean, St Andrews and Gunnamatta. The coastal road from the northern towns is interrupted where the granite hillside meets the waters of Port Phillip Bay at Anthonys Nose, effectively breaking the ribbon pattern of development. McCrae is cradled in these foothills with an exquisite, white sandy foreshore, old lighthouse and historic homestead.

SOUTHERN

Rosebud, Rye and Tootgarook are magnets to holidaymakers and day trippers, offering excellent foreshore facilities, piers, boat launching ramps, entertainment, shops and safe, sandy beaches. Blairgowrie exudes a peaceful, relaxed lifestyle where shallow waters are punctuated by a series of groynes built to restrict the movement of sand. Sorrento, picturesque and dynamic, balances the charm of yesteryear with contemporary eateries and boutiques. Portsea, up-market and exclusive, attracts divers and water enthusiasts to the pier and famous landmark hotel.

Mornington Peninsula National Park is a spectacular, forty-kilometre long, narrow stretch of windswept coastline of pristine beaches and hinterland that separates the wild waters of Bass Strait from the calmer waters of Port Phillip Bay. It runs from the old fort at Port Nepean, historically vital to Melbourne's military defence, past the wild ocean beaches of Portsea, Sorrento, Rye, St Andrews and Gunnamatta to Cape Schanck and Flinders. The surf beach at Gunnamatta is renowned as the most challenging on the Peninsula.

The first settlers landed at Sullivan Bay, Sorrento in 1803 and from the 1840s the Peninsula was exploited for building materials and grazing land. In 1876 the theatrical entrepreneur, George Coppin persuaded local authorities to set aside a coastal strip as an Ocean Park. His paddle-steamer company brought holidaymakers to Sorrento and a steam tram provided transport from the pier to the ocean beach, hence the Coppins name is attached to the lookout, tea-rooms and jetty.

Photo: Sand-sculpting Championship, Rye Foreshore

Eastern Lighthouse, McCrae

White sands and grassed foreshore

McCRAE

McCrae is a small, charming township located opposite the steel lighthouse which was erected in 1883. The 33.5 metre-high lighthouse, with a 120-step spiral staircase, served to guide ships to and from Geelong along the West Channel. It was decommissioned in 1994.

ROSEBUD

Originally called Banksia Point, it was a shipwreck that gave Rosebud its later name. Rosebud's foreshore is characterised by banksia, pine and tea-tree affording cover for the influx of campers over summer. Sandbars are extensive and the water shallow.

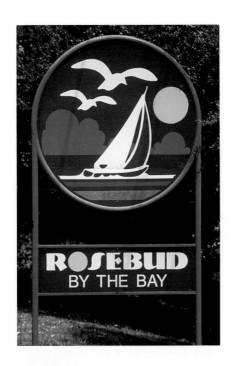

Top Fun Parlour

Rosebud Cinema

Rosebud Pier

ROSEBUD PIER

The deep shipping lane from the Heads runs roughly parallel with the south end of the bay. It is at Rosebud that ships are closest to shore as they turn dramatically at the Hovell Pile heading for Melbourne. The Rosebud Pier provides the ideal vantage point for ship watching.

CAMPERS

In summer the seaside towns face an incoming tide of campers. The foreshores are packed with generations of beachgoers who have booked the same site for decades.

Foreshore camping at Rosebud and Tootgarook

Black Swans, Rosebud

Pelicans, Tootgarook

ICE CREAMS
SOFT DRINKS
WATER
SWEETS
PASTIES
PIES
SAUSAGE ROLLS
POTATO CHIPS
SANDWICHES
CAKE TEA
COFFEE

Beachcomber
CATAMARAN
HIRE & KIOSK
59812112 0401137856
OPEN

TOOTGAROOK

Tootgarook, *land of the croaking frogs*, has a sandy, shallow beach and grassed dunes backed by banksias. Pelicans at the boat ramp appreciate the spoils of a fisherman's catch, usually flathead, whiting or squid.

Rosebud West

RYE BEACHES

Rye is the first bayside town with a bay (front) and ocean (back) beach. The bay beach, with a long stretch of shallow water and white sand attracts windsurfers while families enjoy the diverse foreshore facilities. The rough ocean beach lures surfers eager to challenge the notorious beach considered unsafe for swimming.

Whitecliffs, Rye

Rye Ocean Beach

Summer Carnival, Rye

Mural, Rye Foreshore

Greek Independence Day

The Octopuses Garden, Rye Pier

32

Rye Foreshore

Blairgowrie

BLAIRGOWRIE

Blairgowrie village exudes a peaceful, laidback atmosphere. The front beach is punctuated by a series of groynes, boat-sheds, protective sea wall, Yacht Squadron and Blairgowrie Safe Boat Harbour. The back beaches on Bass Strait include Bridgewater Bay, Pirates Bay, Pearses, Montforts and Dimmicks Beach. At high tide this rugged coast can be enjoyed from spectacular cliff top tracks.

The Bridge, Bridgewater Bay

Dogs Head and Koonya Beach

South Channel Pile Light

Chinamans Hut

Popes Eye

Port Phillip Bay

The Bandstand (1903)

Coppins Jetty, Sorrento Foreshore

38

SORRENTO

Sorrento was the site of Victoria's first official European settlement in 1803. The picturesque seaside town retains the ambience of yesteryear. Nineteenth century limestone buildings and quaint old-fashioned shop fronts are preserved alongside contemporary boutiques and cafes.

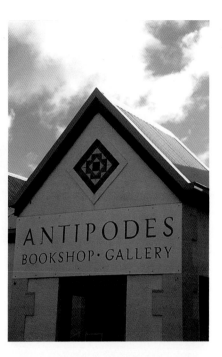

Ocean Beach Road, Sorrento

Australia Day Celebrations, 26 January

Sorrento Sailing Couta Boat Club

COUTA
BOATS

Victoria has the largest Couta boat fleet in the world with the majority in Sorrento. The open wooden sailing boats, around twenty-six feet long, are gaff-rigged with a wide cockpit area originally used for fish storage. Distinctive curved-down bowsprits and white tipped masts typify the inherently stable Couta boats which are now the domain of racing enthusiasts and recreational sailors.

Sorrento Ocean Beach

Coppins Lookout, Sorrento

SORRENTO OCEAN BEACH

The dramatic Amphitheatre is captivating all year round. A famous rock pool exposed only at low tide, offshore rock stacks, surging waves and a magnificent vista in every direction can be enjoyed from within the cosy tearoom or parked car on chilly, windswept days. Summer beach patrols, surf life-saving club, Coppins Track along the cliff top and boardwalk to an historic lookout, ensure each visitor is eager to return.

Sorrento

Shelley Beach, Portsea

PORTSEA

An avenue of cypress trees, cliff top mansions, the 1927 landmark hotel and bustling pier, portray the most westerly town on the Mornington Peninsula. Weeroona Bay is decorated with private jetties and beach boxes and is the destination for beach lovers, divers, fishermen, boats and ferries. In contrast, Portsea Surf Beach, `the place to be seen over summer´, is a long expanse of beach with rips and currents making it dangerous to swim outside the patrolled area.

Port Phillip Bay from Farnsworth Track

London Bridge

Portsea Ocean Beach

Portsea Swim Classic

Portsea Pier

Portsea Surf Beach

Red-brick engine house, Fort Nepean

Quarantine Station

Cattle Jetty, Observatory Point

Point Nepean

SEA PILOTS

The Port Phillip Sea Pilots are responsible for the safe passage of ships through the infamous Rip. For an inbound ship the launch takes the pilot out through the Heads into Bass Strait where a hazardous manoeuvre is required to enable the pilot to climb aboard and take control.

Pilot Launch

The Rip

Diamond Bay, Sorrento

Diamond Bay, Sorrento

St Pauls Beach, Sorrento

Bay of Islands, Sorrento

OCEAN BEACHES

The wild and rugged Bass Strait beaches can be hazardous. Gunnamatta is considered to be the premier surfing spot on the Mornington Peninsula but is perhaps the most dangerous patrolled beach in Australia. St Andrews Beach features a broad expanse of sand, steep slopes, offshore reefs and wave-scoured shoreline. Horses are permitted to canter along this stretch of beach.

Gunnamatta Ocean Beach

St Andrews Ocean Beach

Western Port Bay occupies the eastern side of the Mornington Peninsula extending from Flinders in the south to Yaringa Harbour in the north and includes French Island. The bold, basalt cliffs at Cape Schanck, Fingal, Bushrangers Bay and the Blowhole significantly demarcate the transition from savage Bass Strait seas to the tranquillity of Western Port Bay. This peaceful coast offers a rural, fishing village atmosphere away from the summer crowds that holiday around Port Phillip Bay.

Flinders, Shoreham, Point Leo, Merricks, Balnarring, Somers, Cerberus, Stony Point, Crib Point and Hastings share the same bay and temperate climate but each possesses a character of its own. Flinders retains the air of a relatively undiscovered golfing and fishing resort. Pine trees form the backdrop to Shoreham's main beach distinguishing it from the banksias and coastal tea-tree of its neighbours. Point Leo lays claim to being the closest surf beach to Melbourne and well suited to all levels of ability.

WESTERN PORT

The tiny township of Merricks, with its secluded beach, vineyards and agriculture is in marked contrast to Balnarring which is the second largest town in the Western Port Region. At Somers the pristine beach and bush environment is home, not only to a community that cherishes its privacy, but also to an abundance of koalas and bird life. Central to the town is the historic general store and proximity to Coolart, a 19th century mansion surrounded by gracious gardens and wetlands.

Stony Point is a working port evidenced by the activities of ferries to French Island and Phillip Island, as well as tugs and pilot boats servicing the tankers en route to the industrial plants at Hastings. A fishing fleet, active yacht club and impressive marina give Hastings a busy maritime atmosphere. Western Port Bay has gained world significance for its wetlands and ecological diversity. The walk from Hastings to Jacks Beach includes a long boardwalk crossing the world's southernmost white mangroves.

Photo: Flinders Jetty

Cape Schanck Lighthouse

CAPE SCHANCK

Cape Schanck, on the rugged Bass Strait coastline, is the most southerly point on the Mornington Peninsula. The lighthouse, which is still operational, was built in 1859 from local limestone. The famous timber boardwalk enables access to the beach and rock platform with magnificent views of basalt cliffs, Pulpit Rock and Bushrangers Bay.

Bushrangers Bay

Flinders Jetty

West Head

Farm fresh mussels, Flinders Wharf

FLINDERS

Flinders has retained the peaceful character of an early fishing village. The cliff top affords magnificent views of the picturesque harbour at Kennon Cove across to Phillip Island, The Nobbies and Seal Rocks. West Head marks the point where the calm waters of Western Port meet Bass Strait. Flinders offers both surf and safe beach recreation, diving, fishing and a spectacular century old golf course with sea views from every hole.

HMAS Cerberus

ROYAL AUSTRALIAN NAVY

HMAS CERBERUS located on Hann's Inlet, is the premier training establishment of the Royal Australian Navy with a total Service population of about 1900 members. It also delivers training to personnel from the Army and Airforce. According to Greek mythology, Cerberus signifies the ferocious, three-headed dog-like monster with a serpent's tail that guards the gates to Hades.

The West Head Gunnery Range at Flinders was built in 1959 to fill a need for specialized training and firings with actual gunnery systems fitted in HMA Ships. Live firings are conducted into a dedicated exercise area extending 16 miles into Bass Strait. A full range of practices is possible against air, surface and bombardment targets.

West Head Gunnery School, Flinders

Autumn flowering Pokers

Nobbies View Drought Tolerant Plant Farm

Kniphofia Ensifolia

58

Pines Beach, Shoreham

Gatehouse, Point Leo

Point Leo Surf Life Saving Club

Trigger Bros. Surfing Competition

East Coast Surf School

Grass covered dunes, Point Leo

Thoroughbred training at sunrise, Balnarring Beach

SOMERS

Somers, Balnarring, Merricks, Point Leo and Shoreham are small Western Port towns along the `coast of coves'. Each town has its own character. Somers is surrounded by dense woodland with resident koalas and an abundance of bird life. Footbridges span Merricks Creek, retaining walls protect the Somers foreshore and driftwood gathers along South Beach.

Footbridge, Merricks Creek

Coolart Homestead (c1896), Somers

Ferry from Stony Point to French Island and Phillip Island

Stony Point

French Island

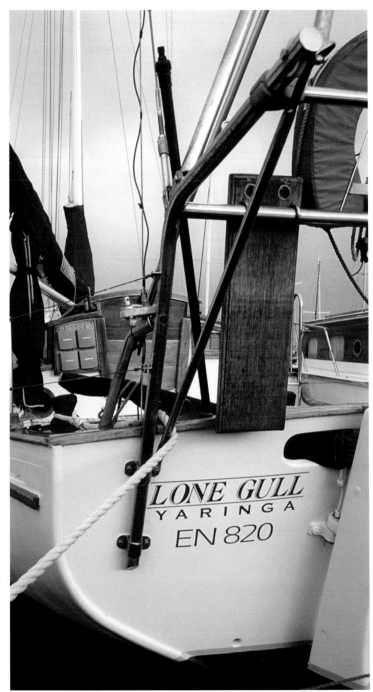

Yaringa Boat Harbour, Somerville

HASTINGS

Hastings, with a deep natural harbour, is the commercial and industrial capital of Western Port attracting Esso and BlueScope Steel (formerly BHP). On a smaller scale, Pelican Pantry on the Hastings foreshore is the new café initiative supported by the Mornington Peninsula Shire. It provides hands-on training experience in hospitality, tourism and retail with employment opportunities for local people.

Sailing, boating, fishing, a marina and yacht club reflect the marine character of the town. Trails to historic Jacks Beach include a boardwalk through white mangroves providing food for an abundant variety of bird and marine life.

Pelican, Hastings Foreshore

Annual Western Port Festival, Hastings

The spectacular hinterland offers a warm welcome and vast array of gourmet delights and experiences. Picture-book landscapes around the delightful hamlets at Red Hill, Main Ridge and Moorooduc have inspired artists for more than a century. The rural surrounds of Somerville, Baxter, Bittern, Pearcedale, Tuerong and Tyabb add to the diversity of the region with market gardens, horse studs and antique stores. Mazes, restaurants, outdoor craft markets and galleries define the perfect destination.

Mornington Peninsula's wine region is rapidly becoming recognised as Australia's leading producer of high-quality maritime, cool climate wines with around 180 vineyards and 50 cellar doors. Local vignerons are renowned for their hospitality and most are in close proximity to each other, making touring and tasting easy. The predominant grape varieties are pinot noir and chardonnay, with smaller plantings of shiraz, cabernet sauvignon, merlot, pinot gris, sauvignon blanc, riesling, semillon and Italian varieties.

The Mornington Peninsula boasts the greatest concentration and variety of quality, year-round golf courses in Australia. Country clubs, links and resort style courses have been built through rolling sand hills. Moonah Links is a spectacular 196-hectare development set in `The Cups´ region. It is home to the Australian Open and has two world-class courses, Legends and Open. Many of the region's golf courses are surrounded by national park with majestic views over Bass Strait and Port Phillip Bay.

HINTERLAND

The scenic drive along country roads and shady lanes delights the traveller with glimpses of ocean. Greens Bush, with an abundance of bird life, native flora and kangaroos, provides an opportunity to appreciate the diverse terrain. An abundance of fresh, seasonal produce – cheese, olives, strawberries, quinces, cherries, apples and chestnuts – is served at local restaurants and can be purchased directly. Country-life festivals and agricultural shows entice the visitor to participate in the friendly, rural community.

Photo: Shearwater, Cape Schanck Resort

RED HILL MARKET

The markets on the Mornington Peninsula, including Red Hill, Mornington, Boneo and Balnarring, showcase the crafts and produce of many talented local people. The Red Hill Community market, established in 1975, is a village style market with hundreds of stalls. Its trademark is `Make it, Bake it, Grow it, Breed it´.

Red Hill Estate

Lindenderry at Red Hill

WINERIES

Mornington Peninsula's vines produce award-winning wines. Bounded on three sides by sea – Port Phillip and Western Port Bays and Bass Strait – the Mornington Peninsula is a unique maritime region where vines thrive in the cool climate that is virtually frost-free. Netting is used to protect the grapes just prior to picking which takes place in autumn.

Red Hill Estate

Stonier Wines, Merricks

Stonier Wines, Merricks

Box Stallion Vineyard, Merricks North

Port Phillip Estate, Red Hill

Vineyards

Country Life Festival

Australian Open Venue, Moonah Links, Rye

Balnarring Picnic Races

Balnarring Market

Red Hill

Boneo

Alpacas, Red Hill

Merricks

Red Hill

Ashcombe Maze & Water Gardens, Shoreham

Cherries

Quinces

Farmers Market, Moorooduc Highway

Strawberries

Regeneration after bushfire, Arthurs Seat State Park

Punty Lane, Shoreham

Greens Bush, Boneo

Koala

Eastern Grey Kangaroos

'Yellow Shoe', Moorooduc

Peninsula Aero Club, Tyabb

YAK-52 Russian design trainer

Mornington Railway Preservation Society, Moorooduc

Frankston developed as a popular holiday resort in the 1890s, a role it has maintained and strengthened. Today Frankston is a delightful all-season destination with wide sandy beaches set against a backdrop of exclusive Olivers Hill, which has been compared to the famous areas of Monterey and Carmel in California. Within a half-hour train ride from Melbourne and twenty-minute drive to the heart of the Mornington Peninsula, Frankston offers infinite lifestyle choices and a dynamic place to live, work and play.

Frankston is one of Victoria's largest regional shopping centres and a vibrant hub of diverse cultural, recreational, entertainment and educational facilities. Monash University, Peninsula Campus is located in Frankston. An impressive cultural drive includes the Frankston Art Centre and Cube 37, Langwarrin Flora and Fauna Park, Ballam Park and Mulberry Hill Homesteads. McClelland Gallery and Sculpture Park are set amid eight-hectares of picturesque bush setting complemented by a central ornamental lake. This outstanding complex, supported by Dame Elisabeth Murdoch, is one of the most important sculpture compilations in Australia.

Long Island is a distinctive feature of Frankston's foreshore. It is girded on one side by the tidal Kananook Creek, running parallel to the coastline, and the other by sea. The spectacular landmark suspension bridge at the entrance to the creek incorporates feature lighting for night viewing and portholes with glass inserts forming a transparent view through the bridge floor.

The popular pier, yacht club and redeveloped Frankston Life Saving Club reflect a proud history, and progressive plans aim to make Frankston a major sailing destination. A raised timber boardwalk, between Olivers Hill and the pier, provides an opportunity to enjoy spectacular views of the foreshore and bay. The distinctive nearby playground is designed on a theme of sand castles emerging and collapsing by the seaside. Frankston is a lively leisure precinct amid water, walks and gardens.

FRANKSTON

Photo: Kananook Creek suspension bridge, Frankston Foreshore

Welcome to Frankston City

Frankston Station

Public Transport

Trains
MET   131 638
Frankston Train Station   9610 6660
Taxi
Frankston Taxi Services   9786 3322
Buses
Frankston and Peninsula Airport Shuttle Bus 9783 1199
Peninsula Bus Lines   9786 7088
770/771 – Frankston to Karingal
772 – Frankston to Eliza Heights
773 – Frankston to Frankston South
774 – Frankston to Delacombe Park
775 – Frankston to Lakewood
778 – Frankston to Pearcedale and Frankston – Orwill Street
779 – Frankston to Belvedere
780 – Frankston to Carrum
781 – Frankston to Mt. Martha

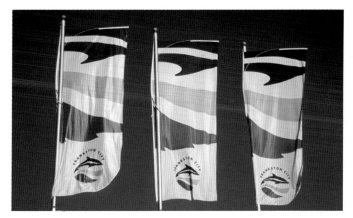

Kananook Creek

Life Saving Club, Frankston Foreshore

Bayside Shopping Centre

Olivers Hill

Frankston Pier

Frankston-Baxter trail sculptures

Boardwalk, Olivers Hill to Frankston Pier

Boathouse, Long Island, Frankston Foreshore

91

Foreshore playground

McClelland Gallery and Sculpture Park

Kananook Creek

Ballam Park Homestead (c 1855)

Monash University Peninsula Campus

Frankston Arts Centre

ACKNOWLEDGEMENTS

Mornington Peninsula is a place that evokes strong affection. It belongs to us all. After a long association with this much-loved area, we appreciate the huge privilege of sharing our personal perspectives through self-publication. With encouragement, patience and support from the following special people, we have confronted many obstacles and shown that dreams are achievable.

We would especially like to acknowledge and thank the following:

Dale Monteith, Ed Monteith, Richard Millott, Ken Derrick, David Kemp, Michael Plumridge, Ian Horton, Meredith Horton, Peter Seal, Patricia Kovacic, Jenny Johnson, Derinda Hoyle, Brian Christensen, Val Christensen, Virginia Juriansz, Phyllis Kailis, Andrew Cotronis, Michelle Bridges, Katie Parkes, Andrew Mackinnon, Alva Hemming, Karen Green, Tim Phillips, Rod Austin, Phil Trigger, Greg Hunt MP, Fraser Bell, Parks Victoria, Malcolm Gordon, Brian Stonier, Dione Wood, Bree Lovell, Alexis Zerbe.

We are forever grateful to Dame Elisabeth Murdoch for enthusiastically encouraging our first publication, *Sea Breeze and Sand*.

Published in 2004
Ides Publishing
PO Box 201
CARNEGIE   3163
VICTORIA   AUSTRALIA
Phone: (03) 9569 7169
E-mail: idespublishing@connexus.net.au

National Library of Australia
Cataloguing-in-Publication data:

Monteith, Anne.
Mornington Peninsula bathed in colour.

ISBN 0-9750912-1-2.

   1.Mornington Peninsula (Vic.) - Pictorial works. 1.
   Dunkley, Bryce Clifford. II Title.

   919.452

Photography by Bryce Dunkley, Anne Monteith
Text by Anne Monteith
Layout and Pre-press by Bryce Dunkley, Anne Monteith, David Kemp
Book and cover design by David Kemp/Cthonic
E-mail: cthonic@bigpond.com

Printed and bound in China
By CTPS through
The Bookmaker
E-mail: bookmake@bigpond.com